LAWRENCE DURRELL was born in India in 1914 and educated at Darjeeling and St Edmund's School, Canterbury. After leading a bohemian life in London for some years, he went abroad, and he has spent most of his life near the Mediterranean. He has worked at the embassy in Cairo, and has been a press officer there and at Athens, and a press attaché in Alexandria and Belgrade. He has been a director of British Council institutes in Kalmata (Greece) and Cordoba (Argentina), and was Director of Public Relations for the island of Cyprus during the troubled fifties. He now writes books at his home in Provence. He is probably best known for *The Alexandria Quartet* (1957–60), a 'word continuum' consisting of the four novels, *Justine, Balthazar, Mountolive* and *Clea,* but it was as a poet that he began writing. His various books of poetry include *A Private Country* (1943), *Cities, Plains and People* (1946), *On Seeming to Presume* (1948), *The Tree of Idleness* (1955), and *Collected Poems* (1950).

ELIZABETH JENNINGS, born at Boston, Lincolnshire, in 1926, was educated in Oxford at the High School and St Anne's College, where she read English. She is a free-lance writer, and describes herself as 'unmarried and a Roman Catholic'. Her books of verse are: *Poems* (1953), which won an Arts Council prize, *A Way of Looking* (1955), which was given the Somerset Maugham Award, *A Sense of the World* (1958), *Song for a Birth or a Death* (1961), *Recoveries* (1964), *The Mind has Mountains* (1966) and *Collected Poems* (1967). In 1961 she also brought out *Every Changing Shape,* a study of 'the relationship between mystical experience and the making of poems', and a translation (in collaboration) of Michaelangelo's sonnets.

R. S. THOMAS was born in Cardiff in 1913. He gained a Latin degree from University College of North Wales at Bangor. He is a clergyman, and was Rector of Manafon, Montgomeryshire, where he wrote many of the poems in *Song at the Year's Turning* (1956), for twelve years between 1942 and 1954. He is now Vicar of Eglwys Fach, Machynllyth, Cardiganshire. Mr Thomas was brought up to speak English, and taught himself Welsh when he was adult. His other collections of poetry are *The Stones of the Field* (1946), *An Acre of Land* (1952), *The Minister* (1953), *Poetry for Supper* (1958) and *Pietà* (1966).

Penguin Modern Poets

I

LAWRENCE DURRELL

ELIZABETH JENNINGS

R. S. THOMAS

Penguin Books

Penguin Books Ltd, Harmondsworth, Middlesex, England
Penguin Books Australia Ltd, Ringwood, Victoria, Australia

—

This selection first published 1962
Reprinted 1963, 1965, 1967, 1969, 1970

—

Copyright © Penguin Books, 1962

—

Made and printed in Great Britain by
C. Nicholls & Company Ltd
Set in Monotype Garamond

Contents

ACKNOWLEDGEMENTS

The poems in this selection are taken from the following books, to whose publishers acknowledgement is made: *On Seeming to Presume* (1948), *The Tree of Idleness* (1955), and *Selected Poems* (1956), by Lawrence Durrell, published by Faber & Faber; *A Way of Looking* (1956), *A Sense of the World* (1958), and *Song For a Birth or a Death* (1961), by Elizabeth Jennings, published by André Deutsch; *Song at the Year's Turning* (1955), and *Poetry for Supper* (1958), by R. S. Thomas, published by Rupert Hart-Davis.

LAWRENCE DURRELL

A Prospect of Children

All summer watch the children in the public garden,
The tribe of children wishing you were like them –
These gruesome little artists of the impulse
For whom the perfect anarchy sustains
A brilliant apprehension of the present,
In games of joy, of love or even murder
On this green springing grass will empty soon
A duller opiate, Loving, to the drains.

Cast down like asterisks among their toys,
Divided by the lines of daylight only
From adventure, crawl among the rocking-horses,
And the totems, dolls and animals and rings
To the tame suffix of a nursery sleep
Where all but few of them
The restless inventories of feeling keep.

Sleep has no walls. Sleep admits
The great Imago with its terror, yet they lie
Like something baking, candid cheek on finger,
With folded lip and eye
Each at the centre of the cobweb seeking
His boy or girl, begotten and confined
In terror like the edges of a table
Begot by passion and confirmed in error.

What can they tell the watcher at the window,
Writing letters, smoking up there alone,
Trapped in the same limitation of his growth
And yet not envying them their childhood
Since he endured his own?

Christ in Brazil

Further from him whose head of woman's hair
Grew down his slender back
Or whose soft palms were puckered where
The nails were driven in,
Rising, denounced the dust they were,
Became white lofts of witness to the sin.

Both here and on that partworn map
The legionary darned for Rome,
Further from Europe even, in Brazil
Warmed by the jungle's sap,
Finding no home from home became
Dark consul for the countries of the Will.

Here named, there honoured, nowhere understood,
Riding over Rio on his cliffs of stone
Whose small original was wood,
In gradual petrifaction of his pain,
He spreads the conscript's slow barbaric stain
Over the cities of the flesh, his widowhood.

Carol on Corfu

I, per se I, sing on.
Let flesh falter, or let bone break
Break, yet the salt of a poem holds on,
Even in empty weather
When beak and feather have done.

I am such fiddle-glib strokes,
As play on the nerves, glance the bare bone
With the madman's verve I quicken,
Leaven and liven body's prime carbon,
I, per se I, alone.

This is my medicine: trees speak and doves
Talk, woods walk: in the pith of the planet
Is undertone, overtone, status of music: God
Opens each fent, scent, memory, aftermath
In the sky and the sod.

O per seo, I sing on.
Never tongue falters or love lessens,
Lessens. The salt of the poem lives on
Like this carol of empty weather
Now feather and beak have gone.

This Unimportant Morning

This unimportant morning
Something goes singing where
The capes turn over on their sides
And the warm Adriatic rides
Her blue and sun washing
At the edge of the world and its brilliant cliffs.

Day rings in the higher airs
Pure with cicadas, and slowing
Like a pulse to smoke from farms
Extinguished in the exhausted earth,
Unclenching like a fist and going.

Trees fume, cool, pour – and overflowing
Unstretch the feathers of birds and shake
Carpets from windows, brush with dew
The up-and-doing: and young lovers now
Their little resurrections make.

And now lightly to kiss all whom sleep
Stitched up – and wake, my darling, wake.
The impatient Boatman has been waiting
Under the house, his long oars folded up
Like wings in waiting on the darkling lake.

'Je Est un Autre'
— RIMBAUD

He is the man who makes notes,
The observer in the tall black hat,
Face hidden in the brim:
In three European cities
He has watched me watching him.

The street-corner in Buda and after
By the post-office a glimpse
Of the disappearing tails of his coat,
Gave the same illumination, spied upon,
The tightness in the throat.

Once too meeting by the Seine
The waters a moving floor of stars,
He had vanished when I reached the door,
But there on the pavement burning
Lay one of his familiar black cigars.

The meeting on the dark stairway
Where the tide ran clean as a loom:
The betrayal of her, her kisses
He has witnessed them all: often
I hear him laughing in the other room.

He watches me now, working late,
Bringing a poem to life, his eyes
Reflect the malady of De Nerval:
O useless in this old house to question
The mirrors, his impenetrable disguise.

Truth

Prospero upon his island
Cast in a romantic form,
When his love was fully grown
He laid his magic down.

Truth within the tribal wells,
Innocent inviting creature
Does not rise to human spells
But by paradox

Teaches all who seek for her
That no saint or seer unlocks
The wells of truth unless he first
Conquer for the truth his thirst.

A Portrait of Theodora

I recall her by a freckle of gold
In the pupil of one eye, an odd
Strawberry-gold: and after many years
Of forgetting that musical body –
Arms too long, wrists too slender –
Remember only the unstable wishes
Disquieting the flesh. I will not
Deny her pomp was laughable, urban:
Behind it one could hear the sad
Provincial laughter rotted by insomnia.

None of these meetings are planned,
I guess, or willed by the exemplars
Of a city's love – a city founded in
The name of love: to me is always
Brown face, white teeth, cheap summer frock
In green and white stripes and then
Forever a strawberry eye. I recalled no more
For years. The eye was lying in wait.

Then in another city from the same
Twice-used air and sheets, in the midst
Of a parting: the same dark bedroom,
Arctic chamber-pot and cruel iron bed,
I saw the street-lamp unpick Theodora
Like an old sweater, unwrinkle eyes and mouth,
Unbandaging her youth to let me see
The wounds I had not understood before.

How could have I ignored such wounds?

The bloody sweeping of a loving smile
Strewed like Osiris among the dunes?
Now only my experience recognizes her
Too late, among the other great survivors
Of the city's rage, and places her among
The champions of love – among the true elect!

A Rhodian Captain

Ten speechless knuckles lie along a knee
Among their veins, gone crooked over voyages,
Made by this ancient captain. Life has now
Contracted like the pupil of an eye
To a slit in space and time for images –
All he has seen of sage and arbutus:
Touched berries where the golden eagle crashes
From its chariot of air and dumb trap:
Islands fortunate as Atlantis was . . .
Yet while we thought him voyaging through life
He was really here, in truth, outside the doorpost,
In the shade of the eternal vine, his wife,
With the same tin plate of olives on his lap.

On Ithaca Standing

Tread softly, for here you stand
On miracle ground, boy.
A breath would cloud this water of glass,
Honey, bush, berry and swallow.
This rock, then, is more pastoral than
Arcadia is, Illyria was.

Here the cold spring lilts on sand.
The temperature of the toad
Swallowing under a stone whispers: 'Diamonds,
Boy, diamonds, and juice of minerals!'
Be a saint here, dig for foxes, and water,
Mere water springs in the bones of the hands.

Turn from the hearth of the hero. Think:
Other men have their emblems, I this:
The heart's dark anvil and the crucifix
Are one, have hammered and shall hammer
A nail of flesh, me to an island cross,
Where the kestrel's arrow falls only,
The green sea licks.

Sarajevo

Bosnia. November. And the mountain roads
Earthbound but matching perfectly these long
And passionate self-communings counter-march,
Balanced on scarps of trap, ramble or blunder
Over traverses of cloud: and here they move,
Mule-teams like insects harnessed by a bell
Upon the leaf-edge of a winter sky.

And down at last into this lap of stone
Between four cataracts of rock: a town
Peopled by sleepy eagles, whispering only
Of the sunburnt herdsman's hopeless ploy:
A sterile earth quickened by shards or rock
Where nothing grows, not even in his sleep,

Where minarets have twisted up like sugar
And a river, curdled with blond ice, drives on
Tinkling among the mule-teams and the mountaineers,
Under the bridges and the wooden trellises
Which tame the air and promise us a peace
Harmless with nightingales. None are singing now.

No history much? Perhaps. Only this ominous
Dark beauty flowering under veils,
Trapped in the spectrum of a dying style:
A village like an instinct left to rust,
Composed around the echo of a pistol-shot.

Delos

FOR DIANA GOULD

On charts they fall like lace,
Islands consuming in a sea
Born dense with its own blue:
And like repairing mirrors holding up
Small towns and trees and rivers
To the still air, the lovely air:
From the clear side of springing Time,
In clement places where the windmills ride,
Turning over grey springs in Mykonos,
In shadows with a gesture of content.

The statues of the dead here
Embark on sunlight, sealed
Each in her model with the sightless eyes:
The modest stones of Greeks,
Who gravely interrupted death by pleasure.

And in harbours softly fallen
The liver-coloured sails –
Sharp-featured brigantines with eyes –
Ride in reception so like women:
The pathetic faculty of girls
To register and utter a desire
In the arms of men upon the new-mown waters,
Follow the wind, with their long shining keels
Aimed across Delos at a star.

The Parthenon

Put it more simply: say the city
Swam up here swan-like to the shallows,
Or whiteness from an overflowing jar
Settled into this grassy violet space,
Theorem for three hills,

Went soft with brickdust, clay and whitewash,
On a plastered porch one morning wrote
Human names, think of it, men became the roads.

The academy was given over
To the investigation of shade an idle boy
Invented, tearing out the heart
Of a new loaf, put up these slender columns.

Later the Parthenon's small catafalque
Simple and congruent as a wish grew up,
Snow-blind, the marbles built upon a pause
Made smoke seem less surprising, being white.

Now syntax settled round the orderless,
Joining action and reflection in the arch,
Then adding desire and will: four walls:
Four walls, a house. 'How simple' people said.

Man entered it and woman was the roof.

A vexing history, Geros, that becomes
More and more simple as it ends, not less;
And nothing has redeemed it: art
Moved back from pleasure-giver to a humour

As with us . . . I see you smile . . .

Footloose on the inclining earth
The long ships moved through cities
Made of loaf-sugar, tamed by gardens,
Lying hanging by the hair within the waters

And quickened by self-knowledge
Men of linen sat on marble chairs
In self-indulgence murmuring 'I am, I am'.

Chapters of clay and whitewash. Others here
Find only a jar of red clay, a Pan
The superstitious whipped and overturned.
Yet nothing of ourselves can equal it

Though grown from causes we still share,
The natural lovely order, as where water
Touches earth, a tree grows up,
A needle touching wax, a human voice.

But for us the brush, the cone, the candle,
The spinning-wheel and clay are only
Amendments to an original joy.

Lost even the flawless finishing strokes,
White bones among the almonds prophesying
A death itself that seemed a coming-of-age.

Lastly the capes and islands hold us,
Tame as a handclasp,
Cause locked within effects, the land –
This vexed clitoris of the continental body,
Pumice and clay and whitewash
Only the darkness ever compromises

Or an eagle softly mowing on the blue . . .

And yet, Geros, who knows? Within the space
Of our own seed might some day rise,
Shriek truth, punish the blue with statues.

Orpheus

Orpheus, beloved famulus,
Known to us in a dark congeries
Of intimations from the dead:
Encamping among our verses –
Harp-beats of a sea-bird's wings –
Do you contend in us, though now
A memory only, the smashed lyre
Washed up entangled in your hair,
But sounding still as here,
O monarch of all initiates and
The dancer's only perfect peer?

In the fecund silences of the
Painter, or the poet's wrestling
With choice you steer like
A great albatross, spread white
On the earth-margins the sailing
Snow-wings in the world's afterlight:
Mentor of all these paper ships
Cockled from fancy on a tide
Made navigable only by your skill
Which in some few approves
A paper recreation of lost loves.

Style

Something like the sea,
Unlaboured momentum of water
But going somewhere,
Building and subsiding,
The busy one, the loveless.

Or the wind that slits
Forests from end to end,
Inspiriting vast audiences,
Ovations of leafy hands
Accepting, accepting.

But neither is yet
Fine enough for the line I hunt.
The dry bony blade of the
Sword-grass might suit me
Better: an assassin of polish.

Such a bite of perfect temper
As unwary fingers provoke,
Not to be felt till later,
Turning away, to notice the thread
Of blood from its unfelt stroke.

The Dying Fall

The islands rebuffed by water.
Estuaries of putty and gold.
A smokeless arc of Latin sky.
One star, less than a week old.

Memory now, I lead her haltered.
Stab of the opiate in the arm
When the sea wears bronze scales and
Hushes in the ambush of a calm.

The old dialogue always rebegins
Between us: but now the spring
Ripens, neither will be attending,
For rosy as feet of pigeons pressed

In clay, the kisses we possessed,
Or thought we did: so borrowing, lending,
Stacked fortunes in our love's society –
Each in the perfect circle of a sigh was ending.

A Bowl of Roses

'Spring' says your Alexandrian poet
'Means time of the remission of the rose.'

Now here at this tattered old café,
By the sea-wall, where so many like us
Have felt the revengeful power of life,
Are roses trapped in blue tin bowls.
I think of you somewhere among them –
Other roses – outworn by our literature,
Made tenants of calf-love or else
The poet's portion, a black black rose
Coughed into the helpless lap of love,
Or fallen from a lapel – a night-club rose.

It would take more than this loving imagination
To claim them for you out of time,
To make them dense and fecund so that
Snow would never pocket them, nor would
They travel under glass to great sanatoria
And like a sibling of the sickness thrust
Flushed faces up beside a dead man's plate.

No, you should have picked one from a poem
Being written softly with a brush –
The deathless ideogram for love we writers hunt.
Now alas the writing and the roses, Melissa,
Are nearly over: who will next remember
Their spring remission in kept promises,

Or even the true ground of their invention
In some dry heart or earthen inkwell?

On Mirrors

You gone, the mirrors all reverted,
Lay banging in the empty house,
Redoubled their efforts to impede
Waterlogged images of faces pleading.

So Fortunatus had a mirror which
Imperilled his reason when it broke;
The sleepers in their dormitory of glass
Stirred once and sighed but never woke.

Time amputated so will bleed no more
But flow like refuse now in clocks
On clinic walls, in libraries and barracks,
Not made to spend but kill and nothing more.

Yet mirrors abandoned drink like ponds:
(Once they resumed the childhood of love)
And overflowing, spreading, swallowing
Like water light, show one averted face,

As in the capsule of the human eye
Seen at infinity, the outer end of time,
A man and woman lying sun-bemused
In a blue vineyard by the Latin sea,

Steeped in each others' minds and breathing there
Like wicks inhaling deep in golden oil.

The Sirens

Trembling they appear, the Siren isles,
Bequeathing lavender and molten rose,

Reflecting in the white caves of our sails
Melodious capes of fancy and of terror,

Where now the singers surface at the prow,
Begin the famous, pitiless, wounded singing . . .

Ulysses watching, like many a hero since,
Thinks: 'Voyages and privations!

The loutish sea which swallows up our loves,
Lying windless under a sky of lilac,

Far from our home, the longed-for landfall . . .
By God! They choose their time, the Sirens.'

Every poet and hero has to face them,
The glittering temptresses of his distraction,

The penalties which seek him for a hostage.
Homer and Milton: both were punished in their gift.

Green Coconuts

At insular café tables under awnings
Bemused benighted half-castes pause
To stretch upon a table yawning
Ten yellow claws and
Order green coconuts to drink with straws.

Milk of the green loaf-coconuts
Which soon before them amputated stand,
Broken, you think, from some great tree of breasts,
Or the green skulls of savages trepanned.

Lips that are curved to taste this albumen,
To dredge with some blue spoon among the curds
Which drying on tongue or on moustache are tasteless
As droppings of bats or birds.

Re-enacting here a theory out of Darwin
They cup their yellow mandibles to shape
Their nuts, tilt them in drinking poses,
To drain them slowly from the very nape:
Green coconuts, green
Coconuts, patrimony of the ape.

On Seeming to Presume

On seeming to presume
Where earth and water plan
No place for him, no home
Outside the confining womb,
Mistake him if you can.
The rubber forceps do their job
And here at last stands man.

Refined by no technique
Beyond the great 'I will',
They pour the poison in,
Confuse the middle ear
Of his tormented dust,
Before the brute can speak
'I will' becomes 'I must'.

Excluded from the true
Participating love
His conscience takes its due
From this excluding sense
His condemnation brought.
From past to future tense
He mutters on 'I ought'.

He mutters on 'I ought'

Yet daring to presume
He follows to the stews
His sense of loathsomeness,
Frustration, daily news.

A scholarship in hate
Endows him limb by limb.
'My mother pushed me from behind,
And so I learned to swim.'

The bunsen's head of hair,
All fancy free and passion,
Till iron circumstance
Confirms him in his lies,
To walk the Hamlet fashion.
He wrings his hands and cries
'I want to live', but dies.

He wants to live but dies.

Return, return and find
Beneath what bed or table
The lovers first in mind
Composed this poor unstable
Derivative of clay,
By passion or by play,
That bears the human label.

What king or saint could guide
This caliban of gloom
So swaddled in despair
To breathe the factory's air,
Or locked in furnished room
Weep out his threescore there
For seeming to presume,

For seeming to presume?

The Prayer-Wheel

Only to affirm in time
That sequence dwells in consequence,
The River's quietly flowing muscle
Turning in the hollow cup
Will teach the human compromise.
Sword and pen win nothing here
Underneath the human floor:
Loved and loving move between
The counterpoint of universes,
Neither less and neither more.

The sage upon his snowy wheel
Secure among the flight of circles
By the calculus of prayer
Underneath the human floor
Founds a commune in the heart.
Time in love's diurnal motion,
Suffering untold migrations,
Islanded and garlanded,
Deep as the ministry of fishes
Lives by a perpetual patience.

Teach us the already known,
Turning in the invisible saucer
By a perfect recreation
Air and water mix and part.
Reaffirm the lover's process,
Faith and love in flesh alloyed,
Spring the cisterns of the heart:

Build the house of entertainment
On the cold circumference
Candle-pointed in the Void.

Cross the threshold of the circle
Turning in its mesmerism
On the fulcrum of the Breath:
Learn the lovely mannerism
Of a perfect art-in-death.
Think: two amateurs in Eden,
Spaces in the voiceless garden,
Ancestors whose haunted faces
Met upon the apple's bruises,
Broke the lovely spell of pardon.

Flower, with your pure assertion,
Mythical and sea-born olive,
Share the indivisible air,
Teach the human compromise:
From a zero, plus or minus,
Born into the great Appearance,
Building cities deep in gardens,
Deeply still the law divines us
In its timeless incoherence.

What is known is never written.
By the equal distribution
He and She and It are genders,
Sparks of carbon on the circle
Meeting in the porch of sex.
Faces mix and numbers mingle
Many aspects of the One

Teach the human compromise.
Speech will never stain the blue,
Nor the lover's occult kisses
Hold the curves of Paradise.

The voices have their dying fall.
The fingers resting on the heart,
The Dumb petitions in the churchyard
Under the European sword
Spell out our tribal suicide.
Grass is green but goes to smoke:
You, my friend, and you, and you,
Breathe on the divining crystal,
Cut down History, the oak:
Prepare us for the sword and pistol.

In Rio (from *Journals of Progress*)

And so at last goodbye,
For time does not heed its own expenditure,
As the heart does in making old,
Infecting memory with a sigh-by-sigh,
Or the intolerable suppurating hope and wish.

It has no copy, moves in its own
Blind illumination seriously,
Traced somewhere perhaps by a yellow philosopher
Motionless over a swanpan,
Who found the door open – it always is:
Who found the fire banked: it never goes out.

We, my dear Melissa, are only typics of
This Graeco-Roman asylum, dedicated here
To an age of Bogue, where the will sticks
Like a thorn under the tongue,
Making our accent pain and not completeness.

Do not interrupt me . . . Let me finish:
Madmen established in the intellect
By the domestic error of a mind that arranges,
Explains, but can never sufficiently include:
Punishes, exclaims, but never completes its arc
To enter the Round. Nor all the cabals
Of pity and endurance in the circus of art
Will change it till the mainspring will is broken.

Yet the thing can be done, as you say, simply
By sitting and waiting, the mystical leap

Is only a figure for it, it involves not daring
But the patience, being gored, not to cry out.
But perhaps even the desire itself is dying.
I should like that: to make an end of it.

It is time we did away with this kind of suffering,
It has become a pose and refuge for the lazy:
As for me I must do as I was born
And so must you: upon the smaller part of the circle
We desire fulfilment in the measure of our gift:

You kiss and make: while I withdraw and plead.

Asphodels: Chalchidice

'No one will ever pick them, I think,
The ugly off-white clusters: all the grace
Lies in the name of death named.
Are they a true certificate for death?'
        'I wonder.'

'You might say that once the sages,
Death being identified, forgave it language:
Called it "asphodel", as who should say
The synonym for scentless, colourless,
        Solitary,

Rock-loving . . .' 'Memory is all of these.'
'Yes, they asserted the discipline of memory,
Which admits of no relapse in its
Consignment, does not keep forever.'
        'Nor does death.'

'You mean our dying?' 'No, but when one is
Alone, neither happy nor unhappy, in
The deepest ache of reason where this love
Becomes a malefactor, clinging so,
        You surely know –'

'Death's stock will stand no panic,
Be beautiful in jars or on a coffin,
Exonerate the flesh when it has turned
Or mock the enigma with an epitaph
        It never earned.'

'These quite precisely guard ironic truth,
And you may work your way through every
Modulation of the rose, to fill your jars
With pretty writing-stuff: but for death –'
    'Truly, always give us

These comfortless, convincing, even, yes,
A little mocking, Grecian asphodels.'

Clouds of Glory

The baby emperor,
reigning on tuffet, throne or pot
in his minority knows hardly what
    he is, or is not,
     sagely he confers
his card of humours like a vane,
veering by fair to jungle foul
     so shapes his course
through variable back to fine again.

    Then
fingers dangle over him: beanstalks.
chins like balconies impend:
kisses like blank thunder bang
    above the little mandarin,
or like a precious ointment prest
from tubes are different kisses
     to the suffrage of a grin.

    He can outface
a hundred generations with a yawn
    this Faustus of the pram,
spreadeagled like a starfish, or
    some uncooked prawn
with pink and toothless mandible
    advance the proposition:
      'I
    cry, therefore I am'

    the baby emperor
    O lastly see

in exile on his favourite St Helena,
corner of a lost playground gazing
    into a dark well,
manufacturing images of a lost past,
expense of spirit in a waste of longing,
    sea-nymphs hourly
    ring his knell.

    small famulus of Time!
born to the legation of our dark unknowing
    the seed was not your
sowing, nor did you make these tall
    untoppled walls
to sit here like a prisoner remembering
    only as a poem now
    the past, the white breasts
that once leaned over you like waterfalls.

A Water-Colour of Venice

Zarian was saying: Florence is youth,
And after it Ravenna, age,
Then Venice, second-childhood.

The pools of burning stone where time
And water, the old siege-masters,
Have run their saps beneath
A thousand saddle-bridges,
Puffed up by marble griffins drinking,

And all set free to float on loops
Of her canals like great intestines
Now snapped off like a berg to float,
Where now, like others, you have come alone,
To trap your sunset in a yellow glass,
And watch the silversmith at work
Chasing the famous salver of the bay . . .

Here sense dissolves, combines to print only
These bitten choirs of stone on water,
To the rumble of old cloth bells,
The cadging of confetti pigeons,
A boatman singing from his long black coffin . . .

To all that has been said before
You can add nothing, only that here,
Thick as a brushstroke sleep has laid
Its fleecy unconcern on every visage,

At the bottom of every soul a spoonful of sleep.

Pomona de Maillol

FOR EVE

An old man tamed his garden with wet clay
Until Pomona rose, a bubble in his arms.

The time and place grow ripe when the idea
Marries its proper image in volition,
When desire and intention kiss and bruise.

A cord passed round the body of the mermaid
Drew her sleeping from the underworld,
As when the breath of resin like a code
Rises from some unguarded still, Pomona
Breathing, surely a little out of breath
The image disengaging from the block,
A little out of breath, and wondering

If art is self-reflection, *who* he was
She woke within the side of, *what* old man
In his smock and dirty cap of cloth,
Drinking through trembling fingers now
A ten year siege of her, the joy in touching
The moistened flanks of her idea with all
An old man's impatience of the carnal wish?

ELIZABETH JENNINGS

Song at the Beginning of Autumn

Now watch this autumn that arrives
In smells. All looks like summer still;
Colours are quite unchanged, the air
On green and white serenely thrives.
Heavy the trees with growth and full
The fields. Flowers flourish everywhere.

Proust who collected time within
A child's cake would understand
The ambiguity of this –
Summer still raging while a thin
Column of smoke stirs from the land
Proving that autumn gropes for us.

But every season is a kind
Of rich nostalgia. We give names –
Autumn and summer, winter, spring –
As though to unfasten from the mind
Our moods and give them outward forms.
We want the certain, solid thing.

But I am carried back against
My will into a childhood where
Autumn is bonfires, marbles, smoke;
I lean against my window fenced
From evocations in the air.
When I said autumn, autumn broke.

Kings

You send an image hurrying out of doors
When you depose a king and seize his throne:
You exile symbols when you take by force.

And even if you say the power's your own,
That you are your own hero, your own king
You will not wear the meaning of the crown.

The power a ruler has is how men bring
Their thoughts to bear upon him, how their minds
Construct the grandeur from the simple thing.

And kings prevented from their proper ends
Make a deep lack in men's imagining;
Heroes are nothing without worshipping,

Will not diminish into lovers, friends.

The Enemies

Last night they came across the river and
Entered the city. Women were awake
With lights and food. They entertained the band,
Not asking what the men had come to take
Or what strange tongue they spoke
Or why they came so suddenly through the land.

Now in the morning all the town is filled
With stories of the swift and dark invasion;
The women say that not one stranger told
A reason for his coming. The intrusion
Was not for devastation:
Peace is apparent still on hearth and field.

Yet all the city is a haunted place.
Man meeting man speaks cautiously. Old friends
Close up the candid looks upon their face.
There is no warmth in hands accepting hands;
Each ponders, 'Better hide myself in case
Those strangers have set up their homes in minds
I used to walk in. Better draw the blinds
Even if the strangers haunt in my own house.'

For a Child Born Dead

What ceremony can we fit
You into now? If you had come
Out of a warm and noisy room
To this, there'd be an opposite
For us to know you by. We could
Imagine you in lively mood.

And then look at the other side,
The mood drawn out of you, the breath
Defeated by the power of death.
But we have never seen you stride
Ambitiously the world we know.
You could not come and yet you go.

But there is nothing now to mar
Your clear refusal of our world.
Not in our memories can we mould
You or distort your character.
Then all our consolation is
That grief can be as pure as this.

In the Night

Out of my window late at night I gape
And see the stars but do not watch them really,
And hear the trains but do not listen clearly;
Inside my mind I turn about to keep
Myself awake, yet am not there entirely.
Something of me is out in the dark landscape.

How much am I then what I think, how much what I
    feel?
How much the eye that seems to keep stars straight?
Do I control what I can contemplate
Or is it my vision that's amenable?
I turn in my mind, my mind is a room whose wall
I can see the top of but never completely scale.

All that I love is, like the night, outside,
Good to be gazed at, looking as if it could
With a simple gesture be brought inside my head
Or in my heart. But my thoughts about it divide
Me from my object. Now deep in my bed
I turn and the world turns on the other side.

Beyond Possession

Our images withdraw, the rose returns
To what it was before we looked at it.
We lift our look from where the water runs
And it's pure river once again, we write
No emblems on the trees. A way begins
Of living where we have no need to beat
The petals down to get the scent of rose
Or sign our features where the water goes.

All is itself. Each man himself entire,
Not even plucking out his thoughts, not even
Bringing a tutored wilfulness to bear
Upon the rose, the water. Each has given
Essence of water back to itself, essence of flower,
Till he is yoked to his own heart and driven
Inward to find a private kind of peace
And not a mind reflecting his own face.

Yet must go deeper still, must move to love
Where thought is free to let the water ride,
Is liberal to the rose giving it life
And setting even its own shadow aside
Till flower and water blend with freedom of
Passion that does not close them in and hide
Their deepest natures; but the heart is strong
To beat with rose and river in one song.

A Fear

Always to keep it in and never spare
Even a hint of pain, go guessing on,
Feigning a sacrifice, forging a tear
For someone else's grief, but still to bear
Inward the agony of self alone –

And all the masks I carry on my face,
The smile for you, the grave considered air
For you and for another some calm grace
When still within I carry an old fear
A child could never speak about, disgrace
That no confession could assuage or clear.

But once within a long and broken night
I woke and threw the shutters back for air
(The sudden moths were climbing to the light)
And from another window I saw stare
A face like mine still dream-bereft and white
And, like mine, shaken by a child's nightmare.

Teresa of Avila

Spain. The wild dust, the whipped corn, earth easy for
footsteps, shallow to starving seeds. High sky at night
like walls. Silences surrounding Avila.

She, teased by questions, aching for reassurance. Calm
in confession before incredulous priests. Then back – to
the pure illumination, the profound personal prayer,
the four waters.

Water from the well first, drawn up painfully. Clinking
of pails. Dry lips at the well-head. Parched grass bending.
And the dry heart too – waiting for prayer.

Then the water-wheel, turning smoothly. Somebody
helping unseen. A keen hand put out, gently sliding
the wheel. Then water and the aghast spirit refreshed
and quenched.

Not this only. Other waters also, clear from a spring or a
pool. Pouring from a fountain like child's play – but the
child is elsewhere. And she, kneeling, cooling her
spirit at the water, comes nearer, nearer.

Then the entire cleansing, utterly from nowhere. No
wind ruffled it, no shadows slid across it. Her mind
met it, her will approved. And all beyonds, backwaters,
dry words of old prayers were lost in it. The water
was only itself.

And she knelt there, waited for shadows to cross the
light which the water made, waited for familiar
childhood illuminations (the lamp by the bed, the
candle in church, sun beckoned by horizons) – but this
light was none of these, was only how the water looked,
how the will turned and was still. Even the image of
light itself withdrew, and the dry dust on the winds of
Spain outside her halted. Moments spread not into
hours but stood still. No dove brought the tokens of
peace. She was the peace that her prayer had promised.
And the silences suffered no shadows.

Fountain

Let it disturb no more at first
Than the hint of a pool predicted far in a forest,
Or a sea so far away that you have to open
Your window to hear it.
Think of it then as elemental, as being
Necessity,
Not for a cup to be taken to it and not
For lips to linger or eye to receive itself
Back in reflection, simply
As water the patient moon persuades and stirs.

And then step closer,
Imagine rivers you might indeed embark on,
Waterfalls where you could
Silence an afternoon by staring but never
See the same tumult twice.
Yes come out of the narrow street and enter
The full piazza. Come where the noise compels.
Statues are bowing down to the breaking air.

Observe it there – the fountain, too fast for shadows,
Too wild for the lights which illuminate it to hold,
Even a moment, an ounce of water back;
Stare at such prodigality and consider
It is the elegance here, it is the taming,
The keeping fast in a thousand flowering sprays,
That builds this energy up but lets the watchers
See in that stress an image of utter calm,
A stillness, there. It is how we must have felt
Once at the edge of some perpetual stream,

Fearful of touching, bringing no thirst at all,
Panicked by no perception of ourselves
But drawing the water down to the deepest wonder.

Letter from Assisi

Here you will find peace, they said,
Here where silence is so wide you hear it,
Where every church you enter is a kind
Continuing of thought,
Here there is ease.
Now on this road, looking up to the hill
Where the town looks severe and seems to say
There is no softness here, no sensual joy,
Close by the flowers that fling me back to England –
The bleeding poppy and the dusty vetch
And all blue flowers reflecting back the sky –
It is not peace I feel but some nostalgia,
So that a hand which draws a shutter back,
An eye which warms as it observes a child,
Hurt me with homesickness. Peace pales and withers.

The doves demure, an English voice divides
The distances. It is the afternoon,
But here siesta has no place because
All of the day is strung with silences.
Bells wound the air and I remember one
Who long ago confided how such ringing
Brought salt into their mouth, tears to their eyes.
I think I understand a mood like that:
Doves, bells, the silent hills, O all the trappings
We dress our plans of peace in, fail me now.
I search some shadow wider than my own,
Some apprehension which requires no mood
Of local silence or a sense of prayer –
An open glance that looks from some high window
And illustrates a need I wish to share.

A Death

'His face shone' she said,
'Three days I had him in my house,
 Three days before they took him from his bed,
 And never have I felt so close.

'Always alive he was
 A little drawn away from me.
 Looks are opaque when living and his face
 Seemed hiding something, carefully.

'But those three days before
 They took his body out, I used to go
 And talk to him. That shining from him bore
 No secrets. Living, he never looked or answered so.'

Sceptic I listened, then
Noted what peace she seemed to have,
How tenderly she put flowers on his grave
But not as if he might return again
Or shine or seem quite close:
Rather to please us were the flowers she gave.

Old Woman

So much she caused she cannot now account for
As she stands watching day return, the cool
Walls of the house moving towards the sun.
She puts some flowers in a vase and thinks
    'There is not much I can arrange
In here and now, but flowers are suppliant

As children never were. And love is now
A flicker of memory, my body is
My own entirely. When I lie at night
I gather nothing now into my arms,
    No child or man, and where I live
Is what remains when men and children go.'

Yet she owns more than residue of lives
That she has marked and altered. See how she
Warns time from too much touching her possessions
    By keeping flowers fed by polishing
      Her fine old silver. Gratefully
She sees her own glance printed on grandchildren.

Drawing the curtains back and opening windows
Every morning now, she feels her years
Grow less and less. Time puts no burden on
Her now she does not need to measure it.
    It is acceptance she arranges
And her own life she places in the vase.

Absence

I visited the place where we last met.
Nothing was changed, the gardens were well-tended,
The fountains sprayed their usual steady jet;
There was no sign that anything had ended
And nothing to instruct me to forget.

The thoughtless birds that shook out of the trees,
Singing an ecstasy I could not share,
Played cunning in my thoughts. Surely in these
Pleasures there could not be a pain to bear
Or any discord shake the level breeze.

It was because the place was just the same
That made your absence seem a savage force,
For under all the gentleness there came
An earthquake tremor: fountain, birds and grass
Were shaken by my thinking of your name.

The Shot

The bullet shot me and I lay
So calm beneath the sun, the trees
Shook out their shadows in the breeze
Which carried half the sky away.

I did not know if I was dead,
A feeling close to sleep lay near
Yet through it I could see the clear
River and grass as if in bed

I lay and watched the morning come
Gentle behind the blowing stuff
Of curtains. But the pain was rough,
Not fitting to a sunlit room.

And I am dying, then, I thought.
I felt them lift me up and take
What seemed my body. Should I wake
And stop the darkness in my throat

And break the mist before my eyes?
I felt the bullet's leaps and swerves.
And none is loved as he deserves
And death is a disguise.

The Annunciation

Nothing will ease the pain to come
Though now she sits in ecstasy
And lets it have its way with her.
The angel's shadow in the room
Is lightly lifted as if he
Had never terrified her there.

The furniture again returns
To its old simple state. She can
Take comfort from the things she knows
Though in her heart new loving burns,
Something she never gave to man
Or god before, and this god grows

Most like a man. She wonders how
To pray at all, what thanks to give
And whom to give them to. 'Alone
To all men's eyes I now must go,'
She thinks 'And by myself must live
With a strange child that is my own.'

So from her ecstasy she moves
And turns to human things at last
(Announcing angels set aside).
It is a human child she loves
Though a god stirs beneath her breast
And great salvations grip her side.

In a Foreign City

You cannot speak for no one knows
Your language. You must try to catch
By glances or by steadfast gaze
The attitude of those you watch.
No conversations can amaze:
Noises may find you but not speech.

Now you have circled silence, stare
With all the subtlety of sight.
Noise may trap ears but eye discerns
How someone on his elbow turns
And in the moon's long exile here
Touches another in the night.

Disguises

Always we have believed
We can change overnight,
Put a different look on the face,
Old passions out of sight:
And find new days relieved
Of all that we regretted
But something always stays
And will not be outwitted.

Say we put on dark glasses,
Wear different clothes and walk
With a new unpractised stride –
Always somebody passes
Undeceived by disguises
Or the different way we talk.
And we who could have defied
Anything if it was strange
Have nowhere we can hide
From those who refuse to change.

Ghosts

Those houses haunt in which we leave
Something undone. It is not those
Great words or silences of love

That spread their echoes through a place
And fill the locked-up unbreathed gloom.
Ghosts do not haunt with any face

That we have known; they only come
With arrogance to thrust at us
Our own omissions in a room.

The words we would not speak they use,
The deeds we dared not act they flaunt,
Our nervous silences they bruise;

It is our helplessness they choose
And our refusals that they haunt.

The Roman Forum

Look at the Forum
Commanded now by Roman pines:
Walk down the ancient paths
Rubbed smooth by footprints in the past and now
Broken among the baths
And battered columns where the lizards go
In zig-zag movements like the lines
Of this decorum.

Not what the man
Who carved the column, reared the arch
Or shaped the buildings meant
Is what we marvel at. Perfection here
Is quite within our reach,
These ruins now are more than monument.
See how the houses disappear
Into a plan

Connived at by
Shadows of trees or light approved
By sun and not designed
By architects. Three columns eased away
From all support are moved
By how the shadows shake them from behind.
The pine trees droop their dark and sway
Swifter than eye

Can catch them all,
O and the heart is drawn to sense,
Eye and the mind are one.

The fragments here of former markets make
(Preserved by the intense
Glare of the Roman unremitting sun),
Such cities that the heart would break
And shadows fall

To see them pass.
Removed from Rome you, half-asleep,
Observe the shadows stray.
Above, the pines are playing with the light.
Dream now so dark and deep
That when you wake those columns, lucid, free,
Will burst like flowers into white
Springing from grass.

My Grandmother

She kept an antique shop – or it kept her.
Among Apostle spoons and Bristol glass,
The faded silks, the heavy furniture,
She watched her own reflection in the brass
Salvers and silver bowls, as if to prove
Polish was all, there was no need of love.

And I remember how I once refused
To go out with her, since I was afraid.
It was perhaps a wish not to be used
Like antique objects. Though she never said
That she was hurt, I still could feel the guilt
Of that refusal, guessing how she felt.

Later, too frail to keep a shop, she put
All her best things in one long narrow room.
The place smelt old, of things too long kept shut,
The smell of absences where shadows come
That can't be polished. There was nothing then
To give her own reflection back again.

And when she died I felt no grief at all,
Only the guilt of what I once refused.
I walked into her room among the tall
Sideboards and cupboards – things she never used
But needed: and no finger-marks were there,
Only the new dust falling through the air.

At a Mass

Waiting restlessly the coming event,
Hearing the three bells ringing the loud warning,
I look for the lifted moment, the lifted cup,
Feeling upon my skin the Roman morning.
I watch with a critical eye the bread raised up
And confuse aesthetics now with a sacrament.

It is the veils drawn over, the decent hiding
That recall the decorum the test of art demands.
Around me the people pray, forgetful of
Even their painful eyes, their well-worn hands.
I struggle now with my own ideas of love
And wonder if art and religion mean dividing.

Each has his way and mine perhaps is to
Suffer the critical sense that cannot rest.
If the air is cool, the colours right, the spoken
Words dramatic enough, then I am pleased.
But why must I ask a sense of style in the broken
Bread and bring God down to my limited view?

Pride enfolds me, pride in the gift of tongues;
Envy too, since I long to be like these
Who approach with empty hands, an open heart –
The simple men lost in simplicities.
I have to endure the ecstatic pain of art
And shape from the silence all my encroaching songs.

To a Friend with a Religious Vocation

FOR C.

Thinking of your vocation, I am filled
With thoughts of my own lack of one. I see
Within myself no wish to breed or build
Or take the three vows ringed by poverty.
     And yet I have a sense,
Vague and inchoate, with no symmetry,
Of purpose. Is it merely a pretence,

A kind of scaffolding which I erect
Half out of fear, half out of laziness?
The fitful poems come but can't protect
The empty areas of loneliness.
     You know what you must do,
So that mere breathing is a way to bless.
Dark nights, perhaps, but no grey days for you.

Your vows enfold you. I must make my own;
Now this, now that, each one empirical.
My poems move from feelings not yet known,
And when the poem is written I can feel
     A flash, a moment's peace.
The curtain will be drawn across your grille.
My silences are always enemies.

Yet with the same convictions that you have
(It is but your vocation that I lack),
I must, like you, believe in perfect love.
It is the dark, the dark that draws me back
     Into a chaos where
Vocations, visions fail, the will grows slack
And I am stunned by silence everywhere.

Two Deaths

It was only a film,
Perhaps I shall say later
Forgetting the story, left only
With bright images – the blazing dawn
Over the European ravaged plain,
And a white unsaddled horse, the only calm
Living creature. Will only such pictures remain?

Or shall I see
The shot boy running, running
Clutching the white sheet on the washing-line,
Looking at his own blood like a child
Who never saw blood before and feels defiled,
A boy dying without dignity
Yet brave still, trying to stop himself from falling
And screaming – his white girl waiting just out of
    calling?

I am ashamed
Not to have seen anyone dead,
Anyone I know I mean;
Odd that yesterday also
I saw a broken cat stretched on a path,
Not quite finished. Its gentle head
Showed one eye staring, mutely beseeching
Death, it seemed. All day
I have thought of death, of violence and death,
Of the blazing Polish light, of the cat's eye:
I am ashamed I have never seen anyone die.

The Counterpart

Since clarity suggests simplicity
And since the simple thing is here inapt,
    I choose obscurities of tongue and touch,
The shadow side of language and the dark
    Hinted in conversations close to quarrel,
Conceived within the mind in aftermaths.
    The intellect no crystal is but swarming
Darkness on darkness, gently ruffled by
    The senses as they draw an image home.

If art must be abstract that needs to speak
In honesty, in painful honesty,
    Then every scene must be composed likewise,
Familiar objects turn to careful shapes,
    Gestures be stiff, emotions emblematic.
So art makes peace with honesty and we
    Detect a blazing, a Byzantine world,
A formal image shining from the dark
    But no less enigmatic than the dark.

Only in such decorum can our pain
Survive without dilution or pretence.
    The agony of loss, the potent thrust
Of seed that never will become a child
    Need the severity of metaphor,
The symbol on the shield, the dove, the lion
    Fixed in a stillness where the darkness folds
In pleated curtains, nothing disarranged:
    And only then the eye begins to see.

Harvest and Consecration

After the heaped piles and the cornsheaves waiting
To be collected, gathered into barns,
After all fruits have burst their skins, the sating
    Season cools and turns,
And then I think of something that you said
Of when you held the chalice and the bread.

I spoke of Mass and thought of it as close
To how a season feels which stirs and brings
Fire to the hearth, food to the hungry house
    And strange, uncovered things –
God in a garden then in sheaves of corn
And the white bread a way to be reborn.

I thought of priest as midwife and as mother
Feeling the pain, feeling the pleasure too,
    All opposites together,
Until you said no one could feel such passion
And still preserve the power of consecration.

And it is true. How cool the gold sheaves lie,
Rich without need to ask for any more
Richness. The seed, the simple thing must die
    If only to restore
Our faith in fruitful, hidden things. I see
The wine and bread protect our ecstasy.

The Diamond Cutter

Not what the light will do but how he shapes it
And what particular colours it will bear.

And something of the climber's concentration
Seeing the white peak, setting the right foot there.

Not how the sun was plausible at morning
Nor how it was distributed at noon,

And not how much the single stone could show
But rather how much brilliance it would shun;

Simply a paring down, a cleaving to
One object, as the star-gazer who sees

One single comet polished by its fall
Rather than countless, untouched galaxies.

Song for a Birth or a Death

Last night I saw the savage world
And heard the blood beat up the stair;
The fox's bark, the owl's shrewd pounce,
The crying creatures – all were there,
And men in bed with love and fear.

The slit moon only emphasized
How blood must flow and teeth must grip.
What does the calm light understand,
The light which draws the tide and ship
And drags the owl upon its prey
And human creatures lip to lip?

Last night I watched how pleasure must
Leap from disaster with its will:
The fox's fear, the watch-dog's lust
Know that all matings mean a kill:
And human creatures kissed in trust
Feel the blood throb to death until

The seed is struck, the pleasure's done,
The birds are thronging in the air;
The moon gives way to widespread sun.
Yes but the pain still crouches where
The young fox and the child are trapped
And cries of love are cries of fear.

Family Affairs

No longer here the blaze that we'd engender
Out of pure wrath. We pick at quarrels now
As fussy women stitch at cotton, slow
Now to forget and too far to surrender.
The anger stops, apologies also.

And in this end of summer, weighted calm
(Climate of mind, I mean), we are apart
Further than ever when we wished most harm.
Indifference lays a cold hand on the heart;
We need the violence to keep us warm.

Have we then learnt at last how to untie
The bond of birth, umbilical long cord,
So that we live quite unconnected by
The blood we share? What monstrous kind of sword
Can sever veins and still we do not die?

A Game of Chess

The quiet moves, the gently shaded room:
It is like childhood once again when I
Sat with a tray of toys and you would come
To take my temperature and make me lie
Under the clothes and sleep. Now peacefully

We sit above the intellectual game.
Pure mathematics seems to rule the board
Emotionless. And yet I feel the same
As when I sat and played without a word
Inventing kingdoms where great feelings stirred.

Is it that knight and king and small squat castle
Store up emotion, bring it under rule,
So that the problems now with which we wrestle
Seem simply of the mind? Do feelings cool
Beneath the order of an abstract school?

Never entirely, since the whole thing brings
Me back to childhood when I was distressed:
You seem the same who put away my things
At night, my toys and tools of childish lust.
My king is caught now in a world of trust.

Greek Statues

These I have never touched but only looked at.
If you could say that stillness meant surrender
These are surrendered.
Yet their large audacious gestures signify surely
Remonstrance, reprisal? What have they left to lose
But the crumbling away by rain or time? Defiance
For them is a dignity, a declaration.

Odd how one wants to touch not simply stare,
To run one's fingers over the flanks and arms,
Not to possess, rather to be possessed.
Bronze is bright to the eye but under the hands
Is cool and calming. Gods into silent metal:

To stone also, not to the palpable flesh.
Incarnations are elsewhere and more human,
Something concerning us; but these are other.
It is as if something infinite, remote
Permitted intrusion. It is as if these blind eyes
Exposed a landscape precious with grapes and olives:
And our probing hands move not to grasp but praise.

R. S. THOMAS

A Peasant

Iago Prytherch his name, though, be it allowed,
Just an ordinary man of the bald Welsh hills,
Who pens a few sheep in a gap of cloud.
Docking mangels, chipping the green skin
From the yellow bones with a half-witted grin
Of satisfaction, or churning the crude earth
To a stiff sea of clods that glint in the wind –
So are his days spent, his spittled mirth
Rarer than the sun that cracks the cheeks
Of the gaunt sky perhaps once in a week.
And then at night see him fixed in his chair
Motionless, except when he leans to gob in the fire.
There is something frightening in the vacancy of his
    mind.
His clothes, sour with years of sweat
And animal contact, shock the refined,
But affected, sense with their stark naturalness.
Yet this is your prototype, who, season by season
Against siege of rain and the wind's attrition,
Preserves his stock, an impregnable fortress
Not to be stormed even in death's confusion.
Remember him, then, for he, too, is a winner of wars,
Enduring like a tree under the curious stars.

Affinity

Consider this man in the field beneath,
Gaitered with mud, lost in his own breath,
Without joy, without sorrow,
Without children, without wife,
Stumbling insensitively from furrow to furrow,
A vague somnambulist; but hold your tears,
For his name also is written in the Book of Life.

Ransack your brainbox, pull out the drawers
That rot in your heart's dust, and what have you to give
To enrich his spirit or the way he lives?
From the standpoint of education or caste or creed
Is there anything to show that your essential need
Is less than his, who has the world for church,
And stands bare-headed in the woods' wide porch
Morning and evening to hear God's choir
Scatter their praises? Don't be taken in
By stinking garments or an aimless grin;
He also is human, and the same small star,
That lights you homeward, has inflamed his mind
With the old hunger, born of his kind.

Song

We, who are men, how shall we know
Earth's ecstasy, who feels the plough
Probing her womb,
And after, the sweet gestation
And the year's care for her condition?
We, who have forgotten, so long ago
It happened, our own orgasm,
When the wind mixed with our limbs
And the sun had suck at our bosom;
We, who have affected the livery
Of the times' prudery,
How shall we quicken again
To the lust and thrust of the sun
And the seedling rain?

An Old Man

Looking upon this tree with its quaint pretension
Of holding the earth, a leveret, in its claws,
Or marking the texture of its living bark,
A grey sea wrinkled by the winds of years,
I understand whence this man's body comes,
Its veins and fibres, the bare boughs of bone,
The trellised thicket, where the heart, that robin,
Greets with a song the seasons of the blood.

But where in meadow or mountain shall I match
The individual accent of the speech
That is the ear's familiar? To what sun attribute
The honeyed warmness of his smile?
To which of the deciduous brood is german
The angel peeping from the latticed eye?

The Cry of Elisha after Elijah

The chariot of Israel came,
And the bold, beautiful knights,
To free from his close prison
The friend who was my delight;
Cold is my cry over the vast deep shaken,
Bereft was I, for he was taken.

Through the straight places of Baca
We went with an equal will,
Not knowing who would emerge
First from that gloomy vale;
Cold is my cry; our bond was broken,
Bereft was I, for he was taken.

Where, then, came they to rest,
Those steeds and that car of fire?
My understanding is darkened,
It is no gain to inquire;
Better to await the long night's ending,
Till the light comes, far truths transcending.

I yield, since no wisdom lies
In seeking to go his way;
A man without knowledge am I
Of the quality of his joy;
Yet living souls, a prodigious number,
Bright-faced as dawn, invest God's chamber.

The friends that we loved well,
Though they vanished far from our sight,

In a new country were found
Beyond this vale of night;
O blest are they, without pain or fretting
In the sun's light that knows no setting.

(From the Welsh of Thomas Williams, Bethesda'r Fro)

Ire

Are you out, woman of the lean pelt,
And the table unlaid and bare
As a boar's backside, and the kettle
Loud as an old man, plagued with spittle,
Or a cat fight upon the stair?
The sink stinks, and the floor unscrubbed
Is no mirror for the preening sun
At the cracked lattice. Oh, the oven's cold
As Jesus' church, and never a bun
Lurks in the larder – Is this the way
You welcome your man from his long mowing
Of the harsh, unmannerly, mountain hay?

The Evacuee

She woke up under a loose quilt
Of leaf patterns, woven by the light
At the small window, busy with the boughs
Of a young cherry; but wearily she lay,
Waiting for the siren, slow to trust
Nature's deceptive peace, and then afraid
Of the long silence, she would have crept
Uneasily from the bedroom with its frieze
Of fresh sunlight, had not a cock crowed,
Shattering the surface of that limpid pool
Of stillness, and before the ripples died
One by one in the field's shallows,
The farm woke with uninhibited din.

And now the noise and not the silence drew her
Down the bare stairs at great speed.
The sounds and voices were a rough sheet
Waiting to catch her, as though she leaped
From a scorched storey of the charred past.

And there the table and the gallery
Of farm faces trying to be kind
Beckoned her nearer, and she sat down
Under an awning of salt hams.

And so she grew, a small bird in the nest
Of welcome that was built about her,
Home now after so long away
In the flowerless streets of the drab town.
The men watched her busy with the hens,
The soft flesh ripening warm as corn

On the sticks of limbs, the grey eyes clear,
Rinsed with dew of their long dread.
The men watched her, and, nodding, smiled
With earth's charity, patient and strong.

Depopulation of the Hills

Leave it, leave it – the hole under the door
Was a mouth through which the rough wind spoke
Ever more sharply; the dank hand
Of age was busy on the walls
Scrawling in blurred characters
Messages of hate and fear.

Leave it, leave it – the cold rain began
At summer end – there is no road
Over the bog, and winter comes
With mud above the axletree.

Leave it, leave it – the rain dripped
Day and night from the patched roof
Sagging beneath its load of sky.

Did the earth help them, time befriend
These last survivors? Did the spring grass
Heal winter's ravages? The grass
Wrecked them in its draughty tides,
Grew from the chimney-stack like smoke,
Burned its way through the weak timbers.
That was nature's jest, the sides
Of the old hulk cracked, but not with mirth.

Cynddylan on a Tractor

Ah, you should see Cynddylan on a tractor.
Gone the old look that yoked him to the soil;
He's a new man now, part of the machine,
His nerves of metal and his blood oil.
The clutch curses, but the gears obey
His least bidding, and lo, he's away
Out of the farmyard, scattering hens.
Riding to work now as a great man should,
He is the knight at arms breaking the fields'
Mirror of silence, emptying the wood
Of foxes and squirrels and bright jays.
The sun comes over the tall trees
Kindling all the hedges, but not for him
Who runs his engine on a different fuel.
And all the birds are singing, bills wide in vain,
As Cynddylan passes proudly up the lane.

Death of a Peasant

You remember Davies? He died, you know,
With his face to the wall, as the manner is
Of the poor peasant in his stone croft
On the Welsh hills. I recall the room
Under the slates, and the smirched snow
Of the wide bed in which he lay,
Lonely as an ewe that is sick to lamb
In the hard weather of mid-March.
I remember also the trapped wind
Tearing the curtains, and the wild light's
Frequent hysteria upon the floor,
The bare floor without a rug
Or mat to soften the loud tread
Of neighbours crossing the uneasy boards
To peer at Davies with gruff words
Of meaningless comfort, before they turned
Heartless away from the stale smell
Of death in league with those dank walls.

Welsh Landscape

To live in Wales is to be conscious
At dusk of the spilled blood
That went to the making of the wild sky,
Dyeing the immaculate rivers
In all their courses.
It is to be aware,
Above the noisy tractor
And hum of the machine
Of strife in the strung woods,
Vibrant with sped arrows.
You cannot live in the present,
At least not in Wales.
There is the language for instance,
The soft consonants
Strange to the ear.
There are cries in the dark at night
As owls answer the moon,
And thick ambush of shadows,
Hushed at the fields' corners.
There is no present in Wales,
And no future;
There is only the past,
Brittle with relics,
Wind-bitten towers and castles
With sham ghosts;
Mouldering quarries and mines;
And an impotent people,
Sick with inbreeding,
Worrying the carcase of an old song.

Soil

A field with tall hedges and a young
Moon in the branches and one star
Declining westward set the scene
Where he works slowly astride the rows
Of red mangolds and green swedes
Plying mechanically his cold blade.

This is his world, the hedge defines
The mind's limits; only the sky
Is boundless, and he never looks up;
His gaze is deep in the dark soil,
As are his feet. The soil is all;
His hands fondle it, and his bones
Are formed out of it with the swedes.
And if sometimes the knife errs,
Burying itself in his shocked flesh,
Then out of the wound the blood seeps home
To the warm soil from which it came.

Bread

Hunger was loneliness, betrayed
By the pitiless candour of the stars'
Talk, in an old byre he prayed

Not for food; to pray was to know
Waking from a dark dream to find
The white loaf on the white snow;

Not for warmth, warmth brought the rain's
Blurring of the essential point
Of ice probing his raw pain.

He prayed for love, love that would share
His rags' secret; rising he broke
Like sun crumbling the gold air

The live bread for the starved folk.

The Lonely Farmer

Poor hill farmer astray in the grass:
There came a movement and he looked up, but
All that he saw was the wind pass.
There was a sound of voices on the air,
But where, where? It was only the glib stream talking
Softly to itself. And once when he was walking
Along a lane in spring he was deceived
By a shrill whistle coming through the leaves:
Wait a minute, wait a minute – four swift notes;
He turned, and it was nothing, only a thrush
In the thorn bushes easing its throat.
He swore at himself for paying heed,
The poor hill farmer, so often again
Stopping, staring, listening, in vain,
His ear betrayed by the heart's need.

Meet the Family

John One takes his place at the table,
He is the first part of the fable;
His eyes are dry as a dead leaf.
Look on him and learn grief.

John Two stands in the door
Dumb; you have seen that face before
Leaning out of the dark past,
Tortured in thought's bitter blast.

John Three is still outside
Drooling where the daylight died
On the wet stones; his hands are crossed
In mourning for a playmate lost.

John All and his lean wife,
Whose forced complicity gave life
To each loathed foetus, stare from the walls,
Dead not absent. The night falls.

Children's Song

We live in our own world,
A world that is too small
For you to stoop and enter
Even on hands and knees,
The adult subterfuge.
And though you probe and pry
With analytic eye,
And eavesdrop all our talk
With an amused look,
You cannot find the centre
Where we dance, where we play,
Where life is still asleep
Under the closed flower,
Under the smooth shell
Of eggs in the cupped nest
That mock the faded blue
Of your remoter heaven.

The Village

Scarcely a street, too few houses
To merit the title; just a way between
The one tavern and the one shop
That leads nowhere and fails at the top
Of the short hill, eaten away
By long erosion of the green tide
Of grass creeping perpetually nearer
This last outpost of time past.

So little happens; the black dog
Cracking his fleas in the hot sun
Is history. Yet the girl who crosses
From door to door moves to a scale
Beyond the bland day's two dimensions.

Stay, then, village, for round you spins
On slow axis a world as vast
And meaningful as any posed
By great Plato's solitary mind.

Song at the Year's Turning

Shelley dreamed it. Now the dream decays.
The props crumble. The familiar ways
Are stale with tears trodden underfoot.
The heart's flower withers at the root.
Bury it, then, in history's sterile dust.
The slow years shall tame your tawny lust.

Love deceived him; what is there to say
The mind brought you by a better way
To this despair? Lost in the world's wood
You cannot stanch the bright menstrual blood.
The earth sickens, under naked boughs
The frost comes to barb your broken vows.

Is there blessing? Light's peculiar grace
In cold splendour robes this tortured place
For strange marriage. Voices in the wind
Weave a garland where a mortal sinned.
Winter rots you; who is there to blame?
The new grass shall purge you in its flame.

Invasion on the Farm

I am Prytherch. Forgive me. I don't know
What you are talking about; your thoughts flow
Too swiftly for me; I cannot dawdle
Along their banks and fish in their quick stream
With crude fingers. I am alone, exposed
In my own fields with no place to run
From your sharp eyes. I, who a moment back
Paddled in the bright grass, the old farm
Warm as a sack about me, feel the cold
Winds of the world blowing. The patched gate
You left open will never be shut again.

A Person from Porlock

There came a knocking at the front door,
The eternal, nameless caller at the door;
The sound pierced the still hall,
But not the stillness about his brain.
It came again. He arose, pacing the floor
Strewn with books, his mind big with the poem
Soon to be born, his nerves tense to endure
The long torture of delayed birth.

Delayed birth: the embryo maimed in the womb
By the casual caller, the chance cipher that jogs
The poet's elbow, spilling the cupped dream.

The encounter over, he came, seeking his room;
Seeking the contact with his lost self;
Groping his way endlessly back
On the poem's path, calling by name
The foetus stifling in the mind's gloom.

The Slave

No offence, friend; it was the earth that did it.
Adam had Eve to blame; I blame the earth,
This brown bitch fawning about my feet.
My skin was a lily once like yours
Before she smirched it with her dirty ways
Blasting its petals with her cruel frost.
O, I would have had the deft tongue
To balance words with the precision
Of a clean stream, fingering stones;
But what could I do? She dragged me down,
Slurring my gait first, then my speech.
I never loved her, there's no ring
Binding us; but it's too late now.
I am branded upon the brow
With muck, as though I were her slave.
My clothes stink, where she has pressed
Her body to me, the lewd bawd,
Gravid as an old sow, but clawed.

Taliesin 1952

I have been all men known to history,
Wondering at the world and at time passing;
I have seen evil, and the light blessing
Innocent love under a spring sky.

I have been Merlin wandering in the woods
Of a far country, where the winds waken
Unnatural voices, my mind broken
By sudden acquaintance with man's rage.

I have been Glyn Dŵr set in the vast night,
Scanning the stars for the propitious omen,
A leader of men, yet cursed by the crazed women
Mourning their dead under the same stars.

I have been Goronwy, forced from my own land
To taste the bitterness of the salt ocean;
I have known exile and a wild passion
Of longing changing to a cold ache.

King, beggar and fool, I have been all by turns,
Knowing the body's sweetness, the mind's treason;
Taliesin still, I show you a new world, risen,
Stubborn with beauty, out of the heart's need.

The Poacher

Turning aside, never meeting
In the still lanes, fly infested,
Our frank greeting with quick smile,
You are the wind that set the bramble
Aimlessly clawing the void air.
The fox knows you, the sly weasel
Feels always the steel comb
Of eyes parting like sharp rain
Among the grasses its smooth fur.
No smoke haunting the cold chimney
Over your hearth betrays your dwelling
In blue writing above the trees.
The robed night, your dark familiar,
Covers your movements; the slick sun,
A dawn **ac**complice, removes your tracks
One by one from the bright dew.

Priest and Peasant

You are ill, Davies, ill in mind;
An old canker, to your kind
Peculiar, has laid waste the brain's
Potential richness in delight
And beauty; and your body grows
Awry like an old thorn for lack
Of the soil's depth; and sickness there
Uncurls slowly its small tongues
Of fungus that shall, thickening, swell
And choke you, while your few leaves
Are green still.

        And so you work
In the wet fields and suffer pain
And loneliness as a tree takes
The night's darkness, the day's rain;
While I watch you, and pray for you,
And so increase my small store
Of credit in the bank of God,
Who sees you suffer and me pray
And touches you with the sun's ray,
That heals not, yet blinds my eyes
And seals my lips as Job's were sealed
Imperiously in the old days.

The Last of the Peasantry

What does he know? moving through the fields
And the wood's echoing cloisters
With a beast's gait, hunger in his eyes
Only for what the flat earth supplies;
His wisdom dwindled to a small gift
For handling stock, planting a few seeds
To ripen slowly in the warm breath
Of an old God to whom he never prays.

Moving through the fields, or still at home,
Dwarfed by his shadow on the bright wall,
His face is lit always from without,
The sun by day, the red fire at night;
Within is dark and bare, the grey ash
Is cold now, blow on it as you will.

In a Country Church

To one kneeling down no word came,
Only the wind's song, saddening the lips
Of the grave saints, rigid in glass;
Or the dry whisper of unseen wings,
Bats not angels, in the high roof.

Was he balked by silence? He kneeled long,
And saw love in a dark crown
Of thorns blazing, and a winter tree
Golden with fruit of a man's body.

No Through Road

All in vain, I will cease now
My long absorption with the plough,
With the tame and the wild creatures
And man united with the earth.
I have failed after many seasons
To bring truth to birth,
And nature's simple equations
In the mind's precincts do not apply.

But where to turn? Earth endures
After the passing, necessary shame
Of winter, and the old lie
Of green places beckons me still
From the new world, ugly and evil,
That men pry for in truth's name.

Index of First Lines

MORE ABOUT PENGUINS

Penguinews, which appears every month, contains details of all the new books issued by Penguins as they are published. From time to time it is supplemented by *Penguins in Print* – a complete list of all our available titles. (There are well over three thousand of these.)

A specimen copy of *Penguinews* will be sent to you free on request, and you can become a subscriber for the price of the postage – 4s. for a year's issues (including the complete lists) if you live in the United Kingdom, or 8s. if you live elsewhere. Just write to Dept EP, Penguin Books Ltd, Harmondsworth, Middlesex, enclosing a cheque or postal order, and your name will be added to the mailing list.

Some other books of poetry published by Penguins are described on the following pages.

Note: *Penguinews* and *Penguins in Print* are not available in the U.S.A. or Canada

THE PENGUIN BOOK OF FRENCH VERSE

(This collection contains a plain prose translation of each poem)

VOLUME 1

To the Fifteenth Century

Edited by Brian Woledge

This volume covers the earliest six hundred years of French poetry. It contains an excellent selection of verse, much of it naturally anonymous, stretching from the *Chanson de Roland* to Francois Villon.

VOLUME 2

The Sixteenth to the Eighteenth Century

Edited by Geoffrey Brereton

A selection covering nearly three hundred years of French poetry from the decline of the medieval influence to the beginnings of Romanticism, including French verse of the Renaissance.

VOLUME 3

The Nineteenth Century

Edited by Anthony Hartley

This century, which includes such names as Baudelaire, Hugo, Rimbaud, and Mallarmé, can rank with the greatest eras of world literature. The poems included have been chosen on their merits and not merely to illustrate historical development.

VOLUME 4

The Twentieth Century

Edited by Anthony Hartley

An introduction to this volume analyses the relationship between modern French verse and English and European literature, and the collection extends from the turn of the century to the present day. It includes Claudel, Valery, Peguy, Aragon, and many others.

BAUDELAIRE

Edited by Francis Scarfe

A poet whose work is so complex and diverse, though apparently so simple and unified, as Baudelaire's is not to be summarized in any convenient formula. Yet many attempts of this kind have been made; they are useful and have to be taken seriously. A modern Dante? This suggestion, first made in 1857 by Thierry, has been discussed and modified by T. S. Eliot, who would be more satisfied with a comparison with Goethe. 'The Swift of poetry,' suggested Lytton Strachey; but they meet only in their disgust, wit, and gloom, and Baudelaire is the bigger of the two. Aldous Huxley called him 'a bored satanist' and Lionel Johnson stated: 'Baudelaire sings sermons.' He has been described as 'the tragic sophist', as 'too Christian', and as a 'Near-Jansenist'.

In this selection Francis Scarfe has placed the poems, for the first time, in a roughly chronological order while trying to preserve the 'cycles' into which they fall. A plain prose translation is appended to each poem.

SOME PENGUIN ANTHOLOGIES

PENGUIN MODERN EUROPEAN POETS

*Günter Grass**

Günter Grass, famous as a novelist, is here presented as a poet in a
selection from his three published volumes. Grass's belief that an
artist, however committed he may be in life, should be only a jester in
art, is admirably practised in these poems in which fantasy, ingenuity
and humour are substitutes for didacticism, and no word, thing or idea
is too sacrosanct to be played with. Even in the recent controversial
political poems, which come close to blurring his division between
life and art, Grass's tremendous zest and sensuous response is felt.

*Vasko Popa**

This is the first collection of poems by Vasko Popa, the leading
Yugoslavian poet, to appear in English translation. A rich poetic
imagination and extreme concentration of language lend special fibre
to the 'new epic' construction of Popa's poems, which are arranged in
cycles. The European standing of a poet who is essentially Yugoslavian derives from his familiarity with the continent's literature and
his patent acceptance abroad. He was recently awarded the Austrian
Lenau prize.

Anna Akhmatova

Anna Akhmatova, who died in 1966, was among this century's greatest Russian poets. Andrei Sinyavsky writes of her: 'From the barest
whisper to fiery eloquence, from downcast eyes to lightning and
thunderstorms – such is the range of Akhmatova's inspiration and
voice.' Richard McKane's moving English translations do justice to a
poet whose famous cycle, 'Requiem', was recognized as a fitting
memorial to the sufferings of millions of Russians under Stalin.

*Not for sale in the U.S.A. or Canada

CHILDREN OF ALBION

Poetry of the 'Underground' in Britain

Edited by Michael Horovitz

Here at last is the 'secret' generation of British poets whose work could hitherto be discovered only through their own bush telegraph of little magazines and lively readings. These are the energies which have almost completely dispelled the arid critical climate of the 'fifties' and engineered a fresh renaissance of 'the voice of the bard' –

The anthology contains many of the best poems of

Pete Brown	Dave Cuncliffe	Roy Fisher	Lee Harwood
Spike Hawkins	Anselm Hollo	Bernard Kops	Tom McGrath
Adrian Mitchell	Edwin Morgan	Neil Oram	Tom Pickard
Tom Raworth	Chris Torrance	Alex Trocchi	Gael Turnbull

– and *fifty* others – from John Arden to Michael X –

It is edited by Michael Horovitz, with a Blakean cornucopia of 'afterwords' which trace the development of oral and jazz poetry – the Albert Hall Incarnation of 1965 – the influences of the great American and Russian spokesmen – and the diverse lyric, political, visioning and revolutionary orientations of these new poets – stretching out of the parochial slumber of old new lines towards the international and archetype; mainstreams of the word.